Pen It

The People's Accounts, Emotions, and
Thoughts of 2020

Volume I

Publications

Treasures from the King

Finding Your Me

A Child's Tenth

When I Grow (Blow) Up

Shaping My Path

Toilet Treats

Writing Your Story

The 52 Experience

.........Pen It
Compiled by Pam Ryans

DEDICATION

This book is dedicated to all lives touched by 2020. Romans 12:15 tells us to Rejoice with those who rejoice; mourn with those who mourn (NIV). Therefore, we acknowledge and honor the words of this passage.

There were many lives lost during this year. Yet, on the other hand, many have rejoiced. So, it is only right to view each situation by its own merits and live according to the times.

CONTENTS

INTRODUCTION

January 1, 2020, began on a Wednesday at midnight. For many, it started with a celebration filled with laugher and high hopes for a prosperous year. Well, that's the perspective of the United States of America. Yet across the globe, January 1, 2020, was just an ordinary day.

Far beyond the US's celebrations or the ordinary days of others, a deadly global pandemic was rapidly growing amid a gut-wrenching racial injustice that has been increasing seemingly forever. The same smiles on many faces masked heart-aching discrimination, avoidance, violence, and non-inclusion. The global COVID-19 and the world-old injustice met face to face in 2020.

The year is only halfway through, and the year 2020 has already experienced its fair share of world-shifting, life-changing events. From the World Health Organization (WHO) announcing the deadly coronavirus' emergence in Wuhan, China, to the tragic death of NBA legendary Los Angeles Laker's basketball player Kobe Bryant; along with his daughter Gianna and seven others, to the stock market crash of 2020, to the brutal police-involved killings of Breonna Taylor, Ahmaud Arbery, and George Floyd and continued fight of the Black Lives Matter movement, to the arrival of the murder hornets in the US, and still, we're just highway.

There are millions of reported deaths and counted births. We've faced church, businesses, and school closings. The hearts, minds, and lives of the people are impacted by triumph and tragedy, and we continue by GOD's grace. Each soul has its own feeling, and each mind has its own perception. "Pen It" Volume One captures the raw emotions and thoughts of real-time accounts.

Pen It

The People's Accounts, Emotions, and Thoughts of 2020

Volume I

Who Am I?
-Rodney Beaty, Jr.-

I am a son
I am a grandson
I am a nephew
I am a cousin
I am a husband
I am a father
I am a brother
I am educated with knowledge and common sense
I am raised to be nothing short of great
I am not the next statistic in AmeriKKKa
I am, who I am.
I am a valuable asset
I am working towards changing my tomorrow
I am a believer of hope
I am, who I am.
I am a threat, but not to society
I am a force to be reckoned with
I am a game changer
And, I am their biggest nightmare
You see, I am a black man
I am a king
Predestined to trap the system that wasnt set up for me
Determined to change the lives of those after me
I am a black man and I am unstoppable!

My People
-Leon Bradshaw-

Why is it that mainstream media, won't report when 13 black
    women are raped
And why is it that it isn't okay for corrupt cops to be taped
I've seen images of the torture of our ancestors, and it's the
    same as today
Because through my eyes Emmitt Till , is the same as Freddie
    Grey
There was a time when I would close my eyes and pretend not
    to see
Or I would close my mind and pretend not even to be
I would walk through my people's pain and say; [fuck it],
Because it wasn't me
But it is me, Because I am every Black man killed in the streets
I am every Black Man disrespected, and disregarded by the
police
I am the little guy with no voice, like the multiple-choice
    questions with no choice
To put it simply we been robbed, raped, and played
And when we got free we were still robbed, and raped but we
    still prayed
I wanna see my history be turned upside right
I wanna meet every single brother and sister of God's divine
    light
I think that I and we dropped the ball on Tamir Rice
Because I and we know that nothing about that case was done
    right
I love my people, but we're. Ore into twerking than hard
working
The white folks buying guns while we drunk and burping
Now we have people dying from poison water in Flint
And that's because most of the elders never knew what
    gentrification meant
Narcus Garvey said; [up, up you mighty race], because he gave
    us spine
So we must represent our place so we won't be left behind
During the shift Melanated people will grow into a change

—

2

Fr everyone else things will remain the same, which means
   they will remain on the 4th plane
No Ka or Brandon no ancestors left for you to shame
And after this chaos we will get order, and if o die trying I will
   die a martyr

The Virus
-Tony O. Harris Brooks-

My Lord, what's happening? Covid-19 is in our world. This culprit is roaming the earth, destroying and killing humanity in its wake. He doesn't care about race, creed, color, or social status. He's coming to rob us of our lives. Everyone is assumed contagious. We are wearing masks to keep the droplets from spreading. How did this pandemic happen? President Trump blames China and bats. China blames America; they say its a biological warfare. Conspiracy theorists say, "The powers that be are reducing the population and bankrupting the economy.

There's a virus-killing black people. Racist cops and vigilante KKK are hanging and choking them out. Horrified, the world protests, "Equalities for all. Black lives matter." Some white people hate black people. Black people just want to be counted as equals among the races. Racism is a virus that has shaken the world since its inception in slavery.

No one wants to admit it exists in the 21st century, but it does. Blacks are treated as the scourge of the earth. They are feared and hated. Socially unaccepted by nations. Marked as a black stain, so they wipe us out.

George Floyd was murdered. Citizens around the world watched via the internet as his life was taken. A dirty cop held his knee on his neck for 8 minutes and 46 seconds. They say, "He resisted arrest." As George struggled to breathe, he cried out loud for his momma. She's been dead. Maybe he saw her as his dying words uttered, "I can't breathe."

"Enough!" the world extolled. Every city, state, and country started marching and protesting equality and justice for all. There are over 10 million confirmed Covid-19 cases, and the numbers are still climbing. The death toll over a half-million with no end in sight. They have been marching day and night since May 25, 2020, the day George Floyd was murdered (over 30 days).

Lord, there is a virus in the land. The 2020 Presidential elections are in November. Trump doesn't care who catches Covid-19 as he campaigns his way to the primary. He just wants full capacity crowds, not wearing masks. To hell with social distancing by 6 feet. Let's just cozy up together. "Help me win the election; I'll make America great again." His actions excite hate and riots. He distorts the truth with words of discrimination. Donald J. Trump wants China to help him win his second term. Russia helped him win the first. Our president has turned the White House into a den of liars and thieves.

Everything Trump does is for self-promotion and self-gain. He doesn't like what the scientists say about fighting Covid-19. He advises untested medical treatment plans like taking hydroxychloroquine, "What do you have to lose?" He thinks the doctors can come up with a vaccine using disinfectants and bleach. He is a traitor, fascinated with Hitler's neo-nazi values of a New World Order. "Come on y'all, let's kill the Jew."
A virus is stalking up and down, roaming around in and out the earth causing discord, a contagion that changes the way we greet one another in brotherly love sealed with a kiss—no more reassuring human hugs or handshakes. The eyes are the windows to the soul. Simple facial expressions are hidden behind the mask. Six-feet distancing, stay in your bubble. Each bubble contained unto itself. "Let's stop Covid-19 from spreading."

There's a virus in the land killing black people. I see the world fighting back in a pandemic. Demonstrations are around the world, proclaiming equality and justice because all lives matter. The world is crying out for the Black Children of God. My Lord, even unto this day, we are persecuted. We are considered, "That damn spot" that must be exterminated. No

—

matter the achievements of the black race, we are considered plain low-life scum not worth one breath.

There's a virus in the land. The prince and powers of the air is lurking in places seen and unseen. Throwing a rock and hiding his hand as he spread his malice. Its venom is seething throughout governments, kingdoms, and principalities. Enacting laws dehumanizing life choking out that, "Damn black spot." Our world protests as millions die from the viruses.

Humanity feels compassion and cry. They heard the still small voice that uttered, "I can't breathe."

What is Justice?
-Arkeshia Brown-

We want Justice! We want it Now!

Words continuously coming from the mouths of many across the world.

Why did this happen to my baby? When will those who are responsible be held accountable?

Senseless killings are happening day after day with no real justice resulting.

Justice is the idea that individuals are held responsible for his/her actions.

Justice is seeing equality from person to person regardless of race, nationality, sexuality, etc.

Justice is helping those who fall down get back up when the world seems to weigh them down.

In this current state, racism, homophobic acts, police brutality is occurring from sunrise to sunset as if it is just another part of the day.

Justice is not having fear to walk down the road.

Justice is not having fear of what could happen when pulled over for a simple citation.

Justice is sending a child to the store for candy and knowing he/she will come back within a few minutes.

Justice is stopping someone from choking the life from your loved ones when he/she says, "I can't breathe."

Justice is more than a word but an action to be seen.

—

Will justice truly be seen?

Justice has many definitions for many; however, is justice happening right now.

Families, strangers, countries, nations, etc. are uniting to take a stance in this inequality circulating around the world to seek justice but most of all to bring light to every issue which has been "swept under the rug."

There is no one true definition of justice; yet, there is a way to seek it.

Prayer is the key. Faith unlocks the door.

Stand strong and believe life will get better.

Justice will come.

Lion's Den
-Jakeyla Carlton-

I'm not Daniel but I've been in that den
I'm not perfect so the Lord knows imma sin
Man, I hope they let them boys free out the pen
I heard the pen may be the new lion's den
Pick up that paper, pick up that pen
Who job is it to teach the men how to be men
Who job is it to prevent us from committing these sins
They don't go to church because of the old hens
Instead they pull up to the club and order a bottle of Hen
Get messed up and commit a life of sin
Then get thrown in a pen
But what about them guys in blue committing all the sins
I mean damn now my patience getting thin
Throw ours in AND celebrate their kill like it's a win
Damn we're living in a lion's den

Juneteenth

We say we want change
But will drop everything we say for some change
They get mad when you say use common sense
But will say anything for them cents
They ain't dropping hints
That's really a brother getting lynched
And not to mention they threw our sisters in a ditch
I'm mad I'm angry I want to set it off up in this bitch
Calm down Keyla lower the pitch
But what if it was your mother, brother, or sister laying in that
    ditch
Or hanging from a tree being lynched
Some say F-it I don't wanna get lynched
Some Say F-it it's not making me rich
But I say F-it let's stand up and hold up our fist.
Happy Juneteenth!

—
9

Enough of This
-Shawn Crawford-

Seems this world been stuck
on a loop, earth spinning
and most stilling falling
for the same thing,

like ants some skins get
treated, but to close to
home as this been
outraged by such
injustices
damn near
impossible
to turn a blind eye,

like a meteor just hit grounds
eruption in the only sound
I can't breathe, blood boils
at such a cry, standing up
is the only option you
have to play out, no
no matter the fashion
STAND UP IS WHAT YOU MUST DO,

Enough is enough
band together is
a must!

Tugging emotions been tugged
on for far too long, pulled this
time and they got way
more than the asked
for, wrong is wrong
no matter who does it,

drip down Justice
like raindrops get

us all wet with
vibration that can
help heal the wound
no more rope wrapped
around the mouths of
those who wish to speak,

burn is what the truth does
and set ablaze is all who
had enough of this
mistreatment, let the world
heal as we head one step
close to what they fear,

United of all colors
sick of what must
change, hold us
accountable
hold them
accountable!

Enough, of this

Names I could shout out
that been slain but see
then the list would run
so long that this poem
will seem like reading
the obituary on Sunday
morning, surprised the
streets don't run red
from black son who
will never get to
go home.

So very true all lives matter
but its only dark skin tones
that seems to be falling
down at basic traffic

stop now ground covered
in chalk and yellow tape
surround a black son's
finally, actions, let
the dirt and tears
fly, war vets are not
the one's who scream
at night from what they have
seen, so many gone
all over the hate of
one's skin so tried
of it all,

the world has no choice but
to take notice when so in
your face it all has become,
a slap on the wrist won't
fill the void like most
time no sir, let there
be justice one this
one, for all the others
ones that just slipped
by; made so it's all
overlooked. Enough is enough!

Seems to me the words
I can't breathe, as been
a seed that has
been growing
to long for
it on day
to break
ground,

Spreading over the whole world,
those ones with muted
thoughts now in
an outrage, no
more hiding it

something must be
done; time for a change
so we all can make it home!

Enough is enough
we are all sick
of this!

Trying Times

This all seems like a
low budget movie got
us all shouting this can't
be real, but here we stand.

Working only to be save
and all our loves one
will be ok and the credits
rolls and all this stuff is over.

What a story those of the
class of 2020; will have to
tells their kids, In many years
from now a lot of us will
still, be in disbelief.

Who knew a time would come
where being masked up
is the only way you can
even enter a place,
all walking around with
only eyes showing, looking
to make connections without
making a sound, learning to
show our moods with our eyes.
Masked up we may have to be
but your message to the
world can still be heard;
masked but never shushed.

Hoping it's not just
away to try to dampen
the sounds of the out
cries of many still
shouting and have been
for so long, muffled
but you still hear the
screams our eyes pour
in such disbelief, of why
this conversation is on
going, enough of this!

So crazy it all feels
got your glasses all fogged
up, trying not to walk into
things, but it's for our safety
right, no one saw any of
this type of life coming.

Kids being born and no
big family gatherings you
can have. Seems so odd
but joy can still be found
and the one's we love
we find a way to
stay save and
still, show love.

So wild the one's we love
can't even be seen when
sick or dying never
thought I see such
a time, only a certain
few can even be at
a funeral close casket
feels odd. Not being able
to see their face one last
time, trying times when
have come to live in

in 2020.
Everyone just wants to feel save
so mask up be conscious
of your surrounding but don't
you dare let that mask remove
the voice of who you are
don't let dare stop speak
 your truth, don't you dare
stop loving the skin you
are in, mask up or down,
love yourself.

Trying times this maybe
but still doing the best
we can band together
and find a common
ground we all can stand
on and pray we all stay
safe and healthy.

Just waiting for these
trying times come to
end and we can get
to find a new normal
because lord knows
things will never be
the same.

He's Alive and Undefeated
-Dionne Edison-

We had worship service using Zoom. It included the Easter program with the children dressed up saying their speeches and singing songs. The devil's plan to empty the church is to no avail. We can worship anywhere and at, anytime. While I have the capacity to do so, I bear witness, tell the story and praise Him. Glory! Hallelujah! In Jesus' name.

We are very blessed. Little if anything is mentioned on the news now about the people who are homeless or migrants or refugees in the midst of this pandemic. The lack of toilet tissue gets more prominence. Folks with shelter, food, clothing, lights, gas, water, access to technology, and yes toilet tissue and working toilets bemoan social distancing like its the end of the world. Imagine being separated from your family, held in a camp that's standing room only, having to drink water from the toilet, and little food. Imagine that and you are a woman still with childbearing abilities or a child separated from family. Imagine you have family who left home months or years ago and you don't know what happened to them People are enduring atrocities of unspeakable porportions.

For weeks now the COVID-19 has been the main topic of conversation. Behind the scenes some very bad stuff is happening. COVID-19 is the least of our worries. The enemy is busy.

You know what? God is in charge. That's great news. Nothing is hid from Him. However, difficult it is for me there are so many people whose life experiences are so horrible that I can't wrap my mind around it.

I pray for those who are hidden from view. I pray for those who are lost physically, mentally and spiritually. I pray for those who have, care and share. I pray for our leaders: governmental, community, and in our homes. I pray for all humanity. Compassion. Peace. Joy. Love. Jesus said, "It is

---

finished." He has risen! May all be blessed as only God can bless. This prayer includes you and your family. In Jesus' name. AMEN

-Brie Fash-

2020 has been crazy! When I think of it, I think of Y2k. When we were all afraid of what would happen New Year's Day year 2000. It started off with the hint of something brewing in China. Then, BOOM, it was here in the US and like many I was skeptical. I work at Ochsner LSU Health Shreveport in Shreveport, LA. I was sure that things would be different. I was blown away as things started to progress.

There is a YouTuber named LovelyTi and she was discussing the Coronavirus before 2020. She was even talking to someone who lived in Wuhan, China where the virus originated, and they were saying that things were bad. They were saying that the Chinese Government was trying to cover up how bad it was. Then there were the stories about how it had taken over Rome, Italy.

I remember going to work that following Monday and feeling on edge about signing in people. News broke that it was in several states now and spreading. Almost immediately our prompts changed in the system to ask patients. "Have you traveled outside the US in the last 30 days? Have you traveled to China in the last 90 days? Experiencing any cough or fever?" I mean in seconds the prompts were added. This is when I realized that this was getting real. In a joking way we asked these questions. We had no idea how real it was about to get.

The weekend had gone by and it was Monday again. I woke up to a very dark Monday morning. Normally there would be some sun out, but I had received a call from my supervisor stating that I needed to come to work much earlier so that I can get screened to enter the building.

"Screened?" I thought to myself. "What could she mean by screened?" There had been pictures by this time circulating on how they were testing to see if people had the virus. A very

LONG swab that reached back so far...seemed like it may touch your brain. I was like, "ABSOLUTELY NOT!" I pondered, "Is this the day I get fired because I will not be complying to have this stick stuck to the back of my brain!!"

Needless to say, when I arrived, there was a very long line outside the front door to get into the building. It was 6:30am. My shift is 7:30am-4:30pm. I wanted to cry as I got closer to the front of the line. Then I noticed that they had nurses with thermometer machines to take our temps and stickers to put on our badge to indicate we had been screened. I was very relieved. Those who had temps had to immediately go to Employee Health and get tested for COVID-19 (Coronavirus).

Things haven't been the same since that day. I sat wondering if I would be laid off. I work in the Gastroenterology Clinic. At first, I liked the idea of going home and not working, but then I remembered that I had so much going on. I was in the middle of publishing my second and relaunching my first book of my series, "Bought For A Price." I was in the middle of learning the Hair Business. Not sure how it would work out for me when almost 80% of hair extensions come from China.

Seems like everything is falling apart at the seams. That is how I remember feeling. The hospital became ghostly empty; just like the streets as Non-essential workers were asked to stay home; I was essential. We were seeing about 8 patients when we would normally see anywhere from 40 to 60 a day. With the census being low they began to think of ways to help us keep our jobs and not be laid off. So, they took us down to 32 hours a week. We had to use our Vacation time to get our complete 40 hours. I didn't have much so I panicked a little. I was also saddened because I plans to use my Vacation time to go to my sorority, Sigma Tau Sigma Sorority, INC.'s, Annual Gala. I had my dressed picked out and all.
That trip was short lived because Georgia was on a lockdown. So, the Gala was canceled. I wouldn't be able to go anyway. Seeing that my state was in the red zone as one of the most infected states. Seems like when people went to Mardi Gras,

someone had the virus there and spread it to everyone! Coronavirus was close. So close 2 of my coworkers, who sit right next to me, got the virus. I prayed. I read Psalms 91 religiously every day. I trusted God that he would keep me safe; and he has.

The next stage were the lockdowns. Everyone was to be quarantined to their homes unless it was necessary to go out and get necessities. Some states shut completely down. Celebrities quarantined, reality shows shut down, other TV shows were put on hold, and sports were shut down; changing entertainment as we know it.

Everything was different, but it seemed to be working. Until Ahmaud Arbery, Breonna Taylor, and most shocking George Floyd. Black Lives Matter! Black Lives Matter! Ahmaud Arbery was gunned down running through his neighborhood for a job. Breonna Taylor was killed by Police while she lay sleeping in her own bed. George Floyd murdered by Police in BROAD DAYLIGHT and on video for all to see.

George Floyd's murder set in motion a chain of events that have completely altered America as we know it. His murderer looked into the camera as he stood on his neck letting him gasp for air. George Floyd yelling out to his mother is what I feel sparked the outrage that ALL American's felt. All people from all different backgrounds and colors marched in peaceful protests; some protests turning into looting due to the wrong crowds joining the peaceful protests.

With the wake of the protests millions marching all over the US, Coronavirus sparked up again and the numbers begin to rise. Here we are, July 2020. The numbers are still rising. We are coming up on a very important election, and the war on racism has begun to grow larger and larger.

My nephew Xavier had been fighting Brain Cancer for almost 4 years. July 10, 2020, he finally laid down his sword, and went home to be with Jesus. My family has taken it so hard.

The sadness that surrounds me is unexplainable and something I have never felt before. This is 2020. One of the worst years I've ever been a part of.

 At this point, I am not sure what else is going to happen. One thing for sure, this feels like Revelations is coming to pass right before our eyes. Still chanting Psalms 91, praying, covering me, my family, and friends. We straddle the fence in a waiting position as things could either get better or worse.

Eviction Notice: Jim Crow
-Tre' Finklea-

Mr. Jim Crow,

This is your final letter of eviction.
You were introduced to America in 1877 to enforce racial
  segregation.
You showed us and the world the darkness and ugliness of the
  hearts of Americans that echoed Their love and commitment
  to the United States of America.
The Civil Rights Act was your message that we were TIRED of
  you and that it was time to go.
But Jim Crow, although the white only and colored only signs
  have been removed.
The residue and stench of your presence still is amongst us.
Your beliefs are now being Promoted through the highest
  office in the land.
Jim Crow, I can say that you allowed us the opportunity to see
  racism but now they hide. Instead of white sheets, they hide
  behind badges, robes, and white coats.
See Jim Crow, we are TIRED of still entertaining you when we
  walk, jog, and shop.
We're tired of pretending not to hear the sly remarks your
  supporters say about our choice of Hair or the latest killing at
  the hands of you.
TIRED, is an understatement of what we're feeling.
And quite frankly, we're tired of being the only ones tired.

Our ancestors blood, sweat, and tears runs deep through the
  very earth you stand on and the Very waters that cover the
  earth.

WE ARE AMERICA, JIM CROW. And we're TIRED OF YOU.
No more will we allow our brothers and sisters to be killed by
  the very hands of the ones Entrusted to protect us.

No more will we allow individuals to look over us because of
  the color of our skin.

No more will we allow you to disrespect our men, women, and children.
Because Jim Crow, you owe us and we demand it. Damn, the forty acres and a mule.
We demand justice, peace of mind, opportunity, freedom, and support.
We too are AMERICA! We built this nation and if we can't have the freedoms that we've been Promised then neither will you.

Our children will not deal with you or your redundant beliefs and practices.
They will be what your ancestors feared most.
We will take our rightful place.
Although, Jim Crow we've been hurt and beaten by you.
We will not retaliate with hate
Instead, we'll continue to do what we've been doing
Saving you. See, truth is Jim Crow, where would America be if it wasn't for people like me?
Can you imagine a life without light bulbs or traffic lights?
Blood banks or HeLa cells?

The torch that began with Fredrick Douglass is still being ignited in the hearts of Black America.
And as long as you're here Jim Crow, the torch will remain lit.
Because although we're tired of your ways and beliefs, we're not tired of the fight.
So here we are again in 2020, Jim Crow telling you once again that you're not welcomed and Will not be tolerated. This is your last letter of notice to get the hell out.

Practicing Self Care During A Crisis!
-Sheila D. Green-

If you take a close look at what is happening in our society, it is apparent that there are two types of pandemics going on; one is COVID-19 and the other one is racism and hatred. Both pandemics are disproportionately affecting African Americans, particularly African American men. Right now, we are living through a period of unprecedented racial hatred. We have to face the harsh reality that millions of us are being treated differently because of the color of our skin. COVID-19 is taking a significant toll on the African American community. The death rates from COVID-19 is higher proportionately in the Black community. These are definitely uncertain times and the two pandemics are having a major impact on our mental health. With all this uncertainty in the air, as people we feel the need to do something, fix something or prevent something from happening. Wanting to do something, doing something or not knowing what to do; causes a tremendous amount of stress and anxiety in our lives. With all that is going on around us, self care gets pushed to the bottom of our to-do lists. And it's during these times, that caring for yourself matters the most.

Here are some suggestions of how to practice self-care during a crisis:

•Take care of your body by staying active. A little bit of exercise goes a long way. Taking a leisure walk in your neighborhood or some activity that will get your heart rate up will help your body reduce the mental and physical impact of stress.

•Watch what you eat. Proper nutrition is a form of self care that tends to quickly be forgotten when things become hectic and overwhelming. Limit your intake of sugars and processed foods and eat more fruits, vegetables and grains. If you are feeling overwhelmed try setting aside some time to meal prep. Taking time to eat healthy is part of taking care of yourself.

•Make sleep a priority. Not getting enough sleep can have a huge impact on how you feel both emotionally and physically. Lack of sleep causes stress, weight gain and other major health issues. Many experts say that getting the proper amount of sleep is one of the best things we can do for our overall health and well-being.

•It's important to stay socially connected. It's a good idea to communicate with one person outside of your home each day. And do not forget to check on those family members and friends who live alone and may be feeling isolated during this time. There is nothing like having good friends and close family members during a time like this. These are the individuals that will keep you grounded and focused on the important things.

•Make an effort to keep work and living spaces free of clutter. Clutter and disorganization causes stress and interferes with your ability to relax mentally and physically.

•Be mindful of your social media consumption. Repeatedly watching or reading negative stories can increase feelings of stress and anxiety. It has been well documented that spending too much time on social media can have a negative impact on your overall health. It is important to unplug as much as you possibly can. Have times during the day or night where social media is not allowed.

•Do not neglect your responsibilities. During times of high stress, you may feel inclined to not do or follow through on the things that you are supposed to do. Actually, you should do the opposite. If you have something planned to do; go ahead and do it! Neglecting important tasks which you have to do can actually lead to more stress. You see, the thing is, if you don't go ahead and do them, those things are still going to be their later on. When you are already stressed out you don't want things to pile up that are just going to cause you more stress later!

•Pray! During times like this there is a lot of fear and anxiety. One of the best antidotes for fear is prayer. Make prayer a part of your daily routine. It will provide peace and decrease your overall levels of stress.

•During times such as these, we may be experiencing more stress, worry and anxiety than usual. If these emotions persist or worsen counseling or therapy may be needed. Those with preexisting mental health conditions should continue with treatment.

•Having an attitude of gratitude Is key during a time of crisis. Being grateful takes the focus off what is going on around you and helps you to appreciate all the good things that are a part of your life.

•Put your mask on first. During the review of emergency procedures, the airline attendants instruct us to put our mask on first and then assist anyone who may be traveling with us. It sounds counterintuitive for those who want to take care of everyone else first. But the airlines understand the concept; that you cannot effectively help others until you have what you need first!

•And last but not least, find something to do each day that makes you happy! Find something to engage in that relaxes you, recharges you, rejuvenates you and brings you joy. Use your imagination. Practice being good to yourself and don't forget to be kind to others.

Self-care is not selfish. A healthier happier you will help you to enjoy and take care of those around you. Remember, self-care is for everyone and everyone should be practicing self-care!

Blessed in the Pandemic 2020
-Denise Marie Hair-

Though this time has been a scare for many
God has yet blessed me with plenty

With viruses and violence growing rapidly
Peace from God has been my prescription, there my joy has
caused me to live ever so happily

Many won't understand this new mindset that I have
But i recommend anyone to reach and grab...
the hand that is ever so close, right there at the tip of your nose

He said the first will be last and the last will be first
That's why it's so important to read the bible and discover your
favorite verse

We are blessed in the Pandemic and so are you
Continue to stand on God's word cause you know it's true

-Laura T. Hurst-

I have grown quite weary of white people attempting to minimize the effects of slavery in the United States by saying that Africans also enslaved their own people.
Yes, nations have historically enslaved people of other nations, even of their own nations.
This system of race-based enslavement in this nation is markedly different from that Africans-enslaved-other-Africans slavery that Confederate defenders like to trot out as an attempt to get a pass on the sins of this nation.
The sheer brutality that the British brought with their system of slavery was unmatched by any other civilization who enslaved other humans.
The unique idea here in the US is that ONLY BLACK PEOPLE CAN BE SLAVES, AND THAT IS BECAUSE THEY ARE BLACK. That kernel of the chattel slavery practice is what drives much of current ideology and policy.
The idea that black people are "less than" is even written in the constitution of this nation, as we were to be counted as 3/5 of a person.
Period.

The National Anthem

O say can you see by the dawn's early light,
People of color suppressed, repressed, depressed in their
 plight?
This is your land, this is my land
Built into wealth by the grunts, moans, and cries of the
 enslaved African.
My country t'is of thee, sweet land of liberty
Your slaves have been emancipated, but we still ain't free.
We the people in order to form a more perfect union,
Refuse to subscribe to freedom's Impending ruin.
We hold these truths to be self-evident
Proud weeds of revolution grow tall in your fields of injustice.
America, America, God shed His grace on Thee
'Cause I won't stop raging and fighting until we are free.

Necessity's Children

Out of the depths of nothing comes Necessity's children.
Conceived in the bed of imagination,
Bathed in the womb of inspiration,
Emerging from the canal of ingenuity
They are born.

And her children are great in number.
They are the vanguards of technology,
The heralds of progress,
The trappings of civilization.

Necessity is the mother of invention
And the Most Wise is the life-giving Father.
The African, a foremost trustworthy vessel, brings form to the
    spirit of innovation.

Necessity's African children have been exiled,
Held hostage, outright stolen for profit and sport.
But today, they are granted manumission by the recognition of
    their true origins.

Come forth Ironing Board, Biscuit Cutter, Lantern,
        Horseshoe, Pencil Sharpener, and Lawn Sprinkler.
Stand proud Fire Escape Ladder, Curtain Rod Support, Lemon
        Squeezer, Fountain Pen, and Clothes Dryer.
Rise up Elevator, Automatic Transmission, Shoe Lasting
        Machine, Steam Boiler, Furnace, and Railway Air
        Brakes.
Loose your shackles Open Heart Surgery, Hinton Syphilis
        Test, Corn Harvester, and Cotton Gin.
Shout for joy Steam Engine Lubricator, Rotary Engine,
        Automatic Traffic Light, Blood Preservation, and Golf
        Tee.
Rejoice Paper, Writing, Science, Mathematics, and Zodiac.
You and all of Necessity's children are released from the
    bondage

Of the myth that you could not issue forth from the genius of
  the black mind.
While history omits the veracity of your origins, I live the
  blanket of silence from your truth.
For in ransoming Necessity's children, I redeem myself and
I emerge free to lay claim to my natural propensity
To give Necessity grandchildren.

LIFE'S TURMOIL
-Pamela Ray Jackson-

Living through this Pandemic of 2020 has been such a life-changing event. It came to us with no warning, bringing turmoil to countless lives near and far. It has impacted our lives and dramatically changed how we live from day today. Silently, COVID-19 has invaded our country, causing unsurmountable grief. Life, as we have known it, may never return again. Seeing and hearing the statistical data on cases is a feeling of disbelief. It is unbelievable, and I feel as though I am living in an alter universe or acting out a part in a movie. In this movie, the suspense expands each day, as we watch in horror the rise of sickness and death. Daily we are prayerful that the impact of this virus will not affect the lives of our very own families or those in our respective communities, that it would leave us as quickly and silently as it swept upon us. Whether it impacts on a small scale or big scale, this silent invader impacts us all. Each one of us has a story to share about what we are going through.

In my life, I watch the stories about families being ripped apart when COVID-19 knocks on the door to claim a life. No matter how hard we try to prepare, we are constantly seeing families whose attempts have failed, seeing fears taking control and causing turmoil in our nation. The media provides explicit details regarding the signs, symptoms, and warnings of what actually happens when a person tests positive for COVID-19. This disease attacks the lungs and renders a person unable to breathe, forcing them to depend on a ventilator as a source to sustain life, as the machine breathes for the patient. Our heroic medical staff takes a pause from their own families to provide around the clock care to assist in keeping other's loved ones alive. Unfortunately, in some cases, those heroic gestures fail, and removal from the ventilator must be performed. To witness a life leaving the body is an awful scene. Due to the severity of this disease, family members are not allowed to be with their loved ones. When the transition to death occurs without family, it can be a lonely and frightening time.

Knowing that your loved one is there is a comforting feeling as the end is near.

Life is filled with different turmoil that becomes a battle to survive for anyone. A major life turmoil that is on my mind during this time is the death of my son. The similarities of COVID bring the realization of all the pain that was felt. My son was infected with bacterial Meningitis. It is a sudden illness that wreaks havoc on the body. It affected his lungs and brain. He was placed on a ventilator to help him breathe. The day he died is etched in my mind. It was such a sudden shock to lose a child with no warning. One day he is here, and the next day he was gone. This tragic day happened on July 22, 1994. One minute the doctors are trying to resuscitate, and the next few minutes, you are told your child is 99% brain dead. How could this be? He was full of life one day and fighting for his life the next. You hear the doctor say, "Your son has 99.9% no brain activity." You know what this means, but you can't comprehend. Even when you hear the words, "He died of BACTERIAL MENINGITIS." My child is gone. How is this possible? What evil thing took him? Just like COVID, it is invisible without a trace. It appears without warning. The most important difference between COVID and Bacterial Meningitis is that we were able to be there for him. He knows we were there. If he had COVID instead, we would not have been able to be there.

Bacterial Meningitis is a serious virus. Aggressive medical care must be exerted to care for a patient with this disease because it progresses fast. The first few hours are critical. A simple blood test would have diagnosed it earlier. The treatment would have been fast-paced, and his survival rate would have been better. I am left with a pain that no medicine can heal. There is an obvious void in my life that only I can comprehend.

On the day of the funeral, I remember wearing a basic black dress. I had this hole in the middle of my body that I thought everyone could see. Corey is gone but will never be forgotten;

---

he gives me the strength to continue on my journey. I STAND TALL, knowing he is always with me, letting me know things are okay. I know with GOD in my life and my son's spirit, I can do all things!!! The meaning of GRIEF for me was this loss, he is gone, but I always remember how important it is to Embrace his memories Forever.

During this Pandemic, my mind is reliving the time and place during the loss of my son. I am living that day over and over in my head each time I turn on the TV or radio and learn of more COVID hospitalizations and death. I know how far this could go and the pain someone will feel with the loss of the loved one. The feeling of helplessness is a true heartbreak. I do not understand why I am seemingly reliving my grief at the place and time in my life, but maybe somehow it is allowing my body to continue to comprehend the loss. When we grieve, it comes in small doses, probably due to our body, mind, and soul trying to process and deal with it. Therefore, sometimes the year passes okay, and other times it hurts like the first day. Grief is a process with some of life's turmoil, but learning to deal and cope makes us stronger. Understanding this Pandemic and how to cope makes us stronger as people. It is not discriminatory and apparent in helping us come together for good, and GOD's blessings will continue to prevail.

On this journey, stay safe, healthy, and strong!

COVID-19
The Lockdown Was a Prophetic Purposed Breakthrough
-Natasha Jones-

On December 31, 2019 a global pandemic caused by a virus shifted the nation both naturally and spiritually. We went from freely working, traveling, visiting family and friends, and fellowshipping in church to strategic order guidelines of social distancing and wearing protective masks daily. Simple things that we commonly overlooked like covering your cough, daily sanitizing or just washing your hands has now become a strong highly recommended and enforced quarantine must for the safety of us all.

This pandemic thus far has infected roughly 10.4 million people around the world and killed more than 507,000 people. Many people, churches, employers, entrepreneurs and church leaders started to become creative by breaking the walls of normal and shifting to the new normal. Most churches began worshipping beyond four walls having outdoor safe worship and having more intimate fellowship settings within the homes via social media platforms. This movement has transformed so many hearts and saved souls by experiencing the most amazing God experience right in the comfort of one's own home.

A lot of prophets, preachers, pastors, teachers, and even false prophets began to develop so many theories, revelations, and reasons as to what caused the pandemic to come upon us. Many were told it was due to the world living in sin, while others were convinced that it was due to the church needing to repent, turn and sin no more so that God can heal the land , stop the spread and cure this pandemic. While all of the opinions, theories, revelations, and sermons were being expounded upon, God was unleashing a breakthrough for many as well as for me in the midst of a lockdown that shifted to my breakthrough.

In this time of a global pandemic, God shifted me to another level in ministry, my identity, my purpose, motherhood, entrepreneurship and wife in waiting mindset. As I began to write in my prophetic journals Habbakuk 2:2 on every beginning page, God began to answer my concerns in the midst of a crisis pandemic. Immediately after his response I knew where to turn when the crisis became the "New Normal". Having the word of God at reach and the holy spirit on the inside of me, it directed me to Psalm 86:7 which declares "When I am in distress I call to you, because you answer me" and in Psalm 27:5 it declares "For in the day of trouble he will keep me safe in his dwelling; he will hide me in the shelter of his sacred ten and set me high on a rock.

That alone assured me that God is always at his best in the midst of a crisis performing signs, miracles and wonders. This is what God has been doing from the beginning and will forever do until the end of time. So instead of having a recession mindset, pity party and a God why attitude, God shifted me to have "A Succession Breakthrough-Creativity and Vision Mindset". My father once again has proven himself faithful as Yeshua who hears and answers my call. And that is why there is power in being in the position of "The Call".

As history records itself during this global pandemic, it may seem that God is hiding himself. I've learned that if I come humbly and continue to humble myself before him, it is then I can expect that God has truly listened to my call and he has not only listened but has responded with fruitful manifestations. God strategically attended to the voice of my prayers, the actions of my obedience, faith, execution, disciplinary accountability, me fasting obediently and faithfully serving others in my purpose . I've learned that obedience is better than sacrifice, so if God wants us to be obedient we have to be obedient to his word. When we are obedient to God, he will open up the windows of heaven and pour us out a blessing in the midst of a crisis.

With that being said, during this pandemic through obedience, much prayer, faith, the love and support of my children Ava, Alacia and J'Lyric , my sister Tiffany, my parents and my amazing leaders Ike Avow Wilson, Chaundra Gore and Jenelle Harris I am now fully walking in my purpose. I am now radio personality for my own kingdom talk show "Kingdom Purpose Talk" that airs every Wednesday 5pm Est on Kingdom Sound Radio Broadcast under the leadership of CEO Ike Avow Wilson. I am now the promotions and marketing recruiter for Kingdom Sound Radio Broadcast and executive promotions and marketing manager for Kingdom Sound Music Project Group. I am purposely pursuing my career as an at home mompreneur of an amazing business "Kingdom Attitude Elite" where I specialize in graphics design, life and relationship coaching, vocal coaching, prophetic journal coaching, elite arm-blessings elite eyewear and clothing apparel.

I became #1 Amazon best selling author for the "Focused & Aligned Anthology" as one of the co-authors under the visionary of Author Chaundra Gore, co-author for "Stepping Into Our Territories Edition 2," under the visionary of Author/CEO of She Exist, Jenelle Harris and also co-author of the "Pen It" book project under the leadership of visionary Pam Ryans. I am fluently walking as the visionary and CEO of "The Power Hour" conference call and visionary and CEO of "The Love Academy". I am now the molestation advocate/visionary for "Speak Up and Speak Out" and am currently pursuing a career to own my own record label "Kingdom Attitude Soundz."

I lost a lot of family and friends during this pandemic because I chose to shift in God's purpose for my life unapologetically. Elevation requires isolation and obedience to shifting and embracing the fact that even in the midst of a famine, there is an abundant great harvest if we "Just Do Kingdom". God is too big, too amazing, too graceful and too miraculous to work according to what man thinks should be. He works according to his will, his way, his word and his divine plans for our lives. He moves strategically according to kingdom expectations, kingdom assignments and kingdom order. He loves us too much to sit back and watch the visions and the purposes he has given us fail on purpose. In life we win or we learn but we never fail. We only fail if we choose to remain in the pit and allow our God given purpose to dry up only because we refused to just do kingdom. God always hears us even though he may not always come when we want him, but you can be sure he is always on time.

As history records today on July 15, 2020, I am a living testimony that God can he will supply every need according to his riches and glory in Christ Jesus. Has it been easy, no! But has it been rewarding, absolutely. I decided that in the midst of a Pandemic God had a Plandemic and if I wanted to see the full manifestations of God unfold in the midst of it all then I must totally activate my faith and put the visions that God gave me into action by serving unconditionally in my God given purpose and identity. Be encouraged on today and know that God can and will always prove himself worthy. Pandemic or Plandemic, all the glory will forever belong to him our amazing Yeshua, my Yahweh!

A Self-Love Awakening
-Mia Monique-

I am no longer the hurt girl who hurts people.

I am awakened at the light of healing and peace.

I am the heat of the rising sun.

The pulse of a revived heart.

The scent of rain after a storm when the sun is about to peak.

I am that breath of fresh air relieved when it was hard to breathe.

I am forgiveness at the end of a bitter grudge.

The girl who was once afraid to love.

I am the sound of a new day.

I am healed

Letter of Gratitude
I've Found My Peace
-Cheryl D. Moore-

It's been so easy to get lost in me,
to lose focus on my purpose when trouble is all I see.

As I sit to clean my lens and clear my mind,
I can't help but run back the things I plan to leave behind.

Four years since Dad died, and I remember trying to find that
hill-on which everyone kept telling me to look.
So many claimed to know how I felt, but this church girl was
  shook.
I questioned everything I was groomed in, everything I knew.
Grace wasn't sufficient in my eyes. Now I think back - and it's
  crazy that You loved me enough to see me through.

Fast forward 2 years and I ease back in a church.
I wanted to doubt in my hurt -but You'd blessed me with too
  much.
So, there I was- being renewed and set free,
feeling like life was finally on an uptick for me.
A month into the rejuvenated me and an accident totaled my
  vehicle, but my life was spared.
I felt the enemy tugging at my Faith but I couldn't go back- I
wouldn't dare.

I found a praise and gave you my thanks, reflected on the
meaning to leave my troubles on the bank of the river. That's
what Mom said - by the riverside.

Another month rolled by and You called my brother home, it
  was so reminiscent of losing my dad,
but as I was applying a little healing to that situation - things
  really got bad.
My brother is gone for 2 weeks and I'm struggling not to
  smother,

39

who knew you'd reach back down and grab my mother?
So much emotion, there's not enough time in the day - but I'm
intentional in looking to you,
I've learned You Are My Way.

It's been a year since that and I long for it all,
talks with Mom, seeing my Dad, or brother with the random
   call.
Now I see that You allowed me to be.
Allowed me to be hurt, allowed me to have loss, allowed me to
   turn away, allowed me to live through it for preparation.

So COVID came, hit 2 of my babies, friends lost work, can't
   assemble for church, lost a friend of 14-years- she didn't die
   but the relationship did, working from home, family
   members laid off.
Whew - that's enough of the reflect!
I've found my Me in You- I'm happy, I straighten my crown as
   I drop those loads, just a Letter of Gratitude
   to You Lord.

2020 is the Year of Perfect Vision!!
-Laqueisha Price-

Yes !!! 2020 has also become a year of uncertainty for many people, myself included at certain times of the day minute and hour. I know that God has plans for my life. I know my life story has not yet been told or unfolded. I trust God in the middle of this pandemic with my life, even when it gets hard. I'm sure we have all had those personal one-on-one moments with God. Lately, God and I have had many one-on-ones. I feel it only natural but best that we release the painful feelings inside us in order to produce. Even though I know this has to happen. The human in me wants to know why?

Meanwhile, I'm speaking life over my life, my children's life, my family's life. Something I have familiarized myself to do in uncertain times such as these. It is so important as nights and days go by, and my anxiety has grown at an all-time high. Most days are good while other days, I struggle with simple tasks such as washing the dishes or combing my daughter's hair. Although on the bright side, I have grown closer to Jesus Christ as most of us have seen so many looking for answers and strength to get through these unprecedented times, as the politics call it. For me, Jesus is where I find my answer and strength. I've also found my Ministry and gifts and talents; I never knew how to operate in. That's more on the bright side of things.

I do wish, at times, my Husband wasn't incarcerated. I never-never, ever-ever imagined going through a pandemic without my better-half. I imagined married-life being hard at times, even being knowledgeable of the situation before the pandemic. I was like aight, I can handle this. A part of me also knew that I could.

The thing is, what is going on is absolutely a shift in the economy that we are all apart of. Is it sad? Yes, depressingly, yes. Who would have ever thought it would come to a point where I have to protect my mind, minute-by-minute, second-by-second, the most powerful thing the human body has. These are facts. The fact of the matter is, if we are going to get through this strongly, we have to protect the one thing we do have control over, and that's our mind. My mindset is open to new opportunities. In times such as now, the mind tends to think about the things that you want to do with your life, the things that you want to accomplish before leaving the natural world. While staying as safe as I can, I'm home most of the time. I'm trying to figure out the new way of building opportunities.

Right before COVID-19, my life had just taken a shift personally. Now I'm learning to adapt to a new norm. I try as much as possible to speak greatness in the atmosphere because I know God is doing a new thing, and it's going to be BIG!!! My mindset right now is one of the most important things to me. Of course, while keeping myself safe and my little ones safe, I feel like everything is going to get better for us and for this country. My hope is that everything gets better as far as COVID-19. I refuse to speak of it even as I write. I pray that God covers us from the devices of man who seek power and control. But, God!

My God is raising up a Kingdom that's going to prepare His people for the New World. I just have to keep my mind fixed on Him and all He has promised me. Now, of course, there are mornings when I wake up, and I'm like God we are in a pandemic we have racism going on more people are seeing it everyone else is witnessing the racism clearly now not just Black people but the whites as we. To see the whites unite with the blacks and understand how hard Black people have had it in the United States of America has been truly a blessing.

Still, it doesn't change the fact that we have been in pain and oppressed far too long in the United States of America (black folks). I know it's going to take decades for our people to transfer from an oppressive mindset to a liberation mindset. I say this just to say that we have been programmed too long, meaning the black culture has been taught from the oppressor, and it's what most blacks know all so well.

While protecting my mind, I choose to become a part of the solution making an impact by teaching and training others on the importance of having a relationship with God as well as have control of your mind. With my gift of speech and my purpose of serving, I pray to not only get through these times but also to help others get through as well. May, I also mention writing helps me escape from the terms of this world and leads me into a wide spread of vision.

I pray you guys enjoy this reading

Yours truly, Laqueisha

-Cynthia Sewell-

2020 has been a rollercoaster of a year for me, and we are only halfway through. It started out great with a trip to Disney World with my husband and daughter. We had a weeklong vacation there. Once back home, I transitioned to a new job (same profession) with another company and working from home. I was nervous and excited all in one for this change. After two weeks of all my excitement, my only brother made his heavenly transition from labor to reward on Jan. 30th. This REALLY turned my world upside down! So sudden, so unexpected, and so devastating! I felt as if God had just turned his back on me and ignored all of my prayers and tears. Yes, this was my brother, but he was more of a father figure since our father's passing in 1992. So yes, I felt like God sucka punched me!! Wait!! What...You allowed this to happen??!! This is not what I prayed for. I specifically asked for healing on this side! Not in Heaven!! Oh yea, I was hurt and very angry.

A few weeks after his funeral, Covid-19 hit the United States with a vengeance. People were getting sick and dying everywhere. Schools, jobs, and businesses were forced to close. I began to look around (still very angry with God) and see His goodness and blessings in my life, as well as my family's lives. You see, I didn't have to worry about not being able to have my brother a fitting Homegoing Celebration in our family's church. Now families were forced to have graveside services only for the loved ones with only 25 people. I didn't have to worry about how my mom would cope with losing her son and best buddy alone, and I didn't have to worry about my daughter being out of school because through it all, the Lord allowed me to be there! He allowed us (all of our family and friends) to celebrate my brother's life together at church. He allowed me to be there to help my mother with her devastating grief, and both my husband and I still have our jobs, not missing one day of pay! I had to step back, take a look around, and tell HIM "Thank You"!

In June, our black community was hit with yet another devastating loss of life, George Floyd! This sent racial tension to an all-time high! With riots in every major city, more and more evidence of police brutality from everywhere! I began to see how many white people (that I live in the community with) were silent, and that bothered me. I'm like...ok God, their silence speaks volumes for me. You see, I already live in a town where prejudice is obvious and try to be swept up under the rug, but I always stay conscious! Never did I say I was surprised at what I was seeing and not seeing from my white community. There's the news of my people losing their lives and being mistreated because of their skin color, and you can work with us, teach our children in the schools and try to call yourselves Christians! Oh, when they close their eyes and see the true skin complexion of the God they claim they love.... SURPRISE! Yes, He will be the same color as the people you disliked and had hatred in your hearts for. Wow, where will your souls live for eternity? You see, I learned a long time ago that God is not a respecter of person. He does not show favoritism or partiality, and the Bible teaches us that we should not either. So, no one race is superior over the other, and God definitely does not love one race more than the other! I'm not saying all white people are prejudice, but when you look around and see what's going on in the world, and you still want to hold on to the racial flags and monuments of this countries history and have a problem when the world stands up and say, Black Lives Matter! Then yes, you people are prejudice or in denial of it!

Yes, the first few six months in 2020 has been so hard dealing with loss, depression, anxiety, and sooo many other emotions from not just me, but from people all over the world. BUT, one thing I know for sure, God ALWAYS gets the Glory!! Look at that Dixie flag, the confederate statues, and all the racial, hate-filled monuments being taken down! Not just in the United States, but all over the world!! The WORLD!! Nobody but GOD! And through it all, it ALL, I can't help but to give Him all of the glory, honor, and praise. You see, there will be justice for all the police brutalities, all injustices and wrongs will be brought to light!

Lord, I thank you for your love, light, grace, mercy, and peace, even in all the chaos and confusion of the world. Thank you for being in control and for being bigger than all things!

I Gotta Tell Someone,
Can Anyone Hear Me?
-DeAndrae R. Sewell I, M.S.C.E-

I "Gotta Tell Someone" is one of my favorite reggae songs. It is sung by a group called UB40. One of the main messages in the song is expressing of feelings. In this case, I would like to express how I feel when it comes to Covid-19 and the Black Lives Matter movement. When thinking about Covid-19, I have an abundance of emotions. When we first heard about this deadly disease in other countries, I never knew it would have such a worldwide impact. Around March 13, we heard our mayor, Walt Maddox, tell us about the first known case in Tuscaloosa County. At that time, I was nervous but not afraid.

Before I go on, let's explore my way of thinking. Anyone who knows me, understands that I have always taken an approach of being a protector as well as a germophobe. I have always taken the necessary approach of making sure I wash my hands and inform my family of doing the same. My children even had a routine when they came home from school. It was something that I prayed over and asked GOD to bless. I felt it was blessed because it worked.

Coming back to my original point, I began to pray and talk to GOD about creating a new plan in terms of how we, as a family, would deal with Covid-19. I was planning on being off for a week and celebrating my wife's birthday, but with the numbers steadily rising, plans changed. So, I did what I felt was best, quarantining while spending quality time with my family. See, in order to understand why this was so important to me, you would have to know what happened prior to Covid-19.

GOD blessed me with a full-time job as well as two part-time jobs that allowed me to teach, as well as, counsel. I worked anywhere from 65-75 hours a week for the last seven years or so. Although we were blessed financially, I missed out on some great quality time with the family. I found where so many people were complaining about not being able to do what they wanted to do. I found perfect peace. Perfect peace meaning knowing that I am at home, family, and loved ones are doing well, and I am getting to do some things that I haven't done in a long time.

The news media was reporting all these negative things about Covid-19, which made me tighten the ropes a little harder. As time went by, I noticed it was May 1st. I had been allowed to work from home due to school being closed for the remainder of the semester. I knew that we were safe because GOD had kept us, and I was blessed to be with my family. Movie nights, family projects, Bible Study, and just sitting around having meaningful conversations were happening at a rate where it became routine and familiar. I was so happy because being at home with my family was the best feeling while I was still gainfully employed.

As the month continued to pass by, another big thing happened. The Black Lives Matter Movement was back in full force. George Floyd was killed by policemen, and it sparked worldwide emotions. People were beginning to speak out, and it caused racism to once again rear its ugly head. For a moment, Covid-19 was not being talked about daily. This is when I began to see how being quarantined in the house started to play a role in the mental psyche of the people I loved. I began to ask questions during our weekly family meetings concerning everyone's mental psyche. I re-instilled to my family that the choices being made was for everyone's safety and reinforced the importance of being healthy. In order to do what you want to do, you have to do what you got to do right now. LIFE is hard enough, and with everything that is going on in the world today, I can see how it plays a role in emotions. I have two sons and a daughter as well as loved ones who we pray for daily. I am not just speaking about health, but daily social life when it comes to what they may face by being African Americans. During this time, we as parents have a chance to educate our children more about social issues and the issues they may face in the future.

On May 22, my uncle passed away. I could not be there for my grandmother the way I wanted to because of the social distancing law that was in effect. I called, and I prayed as much as possible. On top of that, I had a cousin who was diagnosed with Covid-19. She fought as long as she could before she passed away. The hurt from losing family members back to back made me tighten the reigns a little more. (As you read this, you probably think that I think I am some type of controller.) I LOVE my family harder than anything in this world.

I pray about direction before I decide on anything. I always ask GOD to help me and bless what we are doing as a family. You read about people dying from Covid-19 and also see it on television, but having it happen in your family plays a major role on the thought process. See, all I know to do is to protect my family at ALL costs. This means making the necessary choices about having tons of people visiting, going on vacations, and hanging out just because I am bored. Making the difficult choices now allows you to be able to have fun later. This is not the time to ease up because we are bored. Cases are steadily going up, and you have some people who still do not believe this is something serious. I have always believed that you can always ease up, but it is hard to tightened up. GOD has kept us, and I am so thankful for what he has done.

"I GOTTA TELL SOMEONE, CAN ANYONE HEAR ME" is me expressing to people that I have been affected by what is going on in the world just as much as the next person. What has helped me deal with what is going on is prayer and believing that eventually, we will get back to normalcy. Being with my loved ones has been the best feeling in the world. I feel that GOD wanted us as people to get back to the basics. Getting back to the basics are things such as spending time with loved ones. Time is one of the main reasons why we put family time

---

on the back burner. So, having all this extra time gives us a chance to seek him. If my people, which are called by my name, shall humble themselves, and pray, and seek my face, and turn from their wicked ways; then will I hear from heaven, and will forgive their sin, and will heal their land. 2 Chronicles 7:14.

After all of this is over, we will be able to take that vacation or hang out with friends. If you were laid off or lost a job, GOD will give you a better job. Working from home has helped me realize that I needed to reevaluate my work schedule. We have been able to get things done around the house that we have put off for years. I am so thankful for what GOD has done, doing, and going to do in the future. I know how bad it looks worldwide, but if we seek GOD and stand on his Word, we will be alright. Standing on his Word does not mean praying and then going out doing something stupid. Standing on his Word means doing the right thing while asking GOD to bless and protect you.

At the end of the day, make sure you take advantage of the time you have with family and stress the importance of being together. After all, family is the oldest institute in the world.

BIG LOVE and GOD BLESS!!!!

COVID-19
I Want My Peace of Mind Back
-Debbie L. Sewell-

Ever since the word Coronavirus (COVID-19) has come into the lives of people, the devil has tried to plant the seed of fear into our lives. Fearing for our lives, as well as fearing for our loved ones and friends. Fear that one day we will find ourselves fighting to live. Speaking from experience, I was fearful for many weeks. Who wants to live in fear daily? My motto in life has always been above all else, but let me have my peace of mind. So, when COVID-19 came, I found myself trying to find that place where my peace of mind had gone. So, what did I finally do?

I finally realized that COVID-19 could not come and destroy the relationship that I have with GOD. GOD is a GOD of peace, not of fear. I found that place where you can surround yourself with GOD's peace in the scriptures and song. Daily watching the news and talking with people can cause your beliefs to weaken. Many people feel the virus is not going to get better anytime soon, so COVID-19 tends to have the ability to conquer your mind, as well as your soul.

I beg to differ; one of the hardest things I have come to accept is not being able to spend quality time with your family and friends. Also, not being able to fellowship with your church family will give you a very depressive state of mind. How do you deal with that fear? We must turn to the word of GOD. We must bring to our remembrance the scripture Hebrew 13:5. "I will never leave thee, nor forsake thee." I also try to remember that GOD allowed this virus to come into existence because he has a divine plan. I also know that he brought us to it; he will surely bring us out of it.

When will this happen? We ask ourselves. Only when his purpose and plans have been fulfilled. So, again we ask ourselves, what are his plans and purposes? We may not know

now, but if we would only use our time wisely that he has given us, everything will become clear enough for us to understand. For example, we as people felt we had to be at every event, church program, and funeral service even if we did not know the family. GOD is telling us to be still and concentrate on him. He wants us to concentrate on your own household and immediate family. He wants us to take care of your husband, wife, and children. "The outside world will be there when I am finished working."

I have been reminded that I do not control my life. COVID-19 is a bad thing, but there are good gifts that GOD can bring from this. As I close, John 14:27 says, "Peace I leave with you: my peace I give you. I do not give to you as the world gives. Do not let your hearts be troubled and do not be afraid." The world cannot give you peace in the time of trouble, but if we depend on the Lord in everything we do, everything will be alright.

The Turn Up
-LaKisha Sewell, M.S-

The "Turn up" was real. This is a phrase we often hear the younger generation say. This phrase meant "we had a good time." Since the pandemic, families went from rushing out the door every morning and forgetting to give kids their lunch money, to now sleeping until 2 pm. Our lives as we knew it has been turned upside down. The turn up for some family has been extremely hard mentally, emotionally, financially, physically, and spiritually. We have faced a different challenge every month since the beginning of 2020.

Here is a little look into my life since March 13th. It was Spring Break for the kids. They were super excited to have a break from school. Our youngest was so excited when I picked him up from the afterschool program. He yelled, "finally," when I walked through the door. What he thought was a week-long vacation from school, turned into him finishing the remainder of the year at home.

On that day, it was nothing but excitement in our household. My husband and kids were officially on Spring Break. I looked forward to only getting myself ready for work the following week, and of course, it was my birthday week as well. I was turning the BIG 40! We had planned a big 80's Throwback for the following weekend. Deposits made, food ordered, outfits delivered, and invitations mailed out. This was going to be a party to remember. Yes, it was! The turn up I imagined was filled with music, food, and laughter. Sadly, by that Sunday, Covid-19 was spreading rapidly. The next day, I was faced with canceling my 40th birthday. So, the dis-invites were texted out with a heavy heart. At that point, I thought, "well, things could be worse," especially after getting the deposits back.

I remained optimistic during the following weeks. We spent a lot of time playing in-house games, eating everything sticky and greasy, and sleeping in. My husband and I were able to spend quality time together with minimal disagreements. Life was really feeling like a real good ole turn up. By the end of March, I was told some very disappointing news that I would be temporarily laid off due to the increasing numbers of Covid-19 cases. My husband was forced to work from home. He was excited for that news, especially since he has worked three jobs for the last seven years or so. The kids were excited to be home but hated the fact that they had to do their schoolwork at home. Second stated once, after refusing to do any more math, "The people at school is trying to mess up my life!"

We had created a routine, and they knew it was important for them to finish the school year strong even while during their schoolwork from home. After completing several house projects, online shopping, zoom parties, Bible studies, and eating homecooked meals, the turn up started turning down for us. The kids wanted to get out of the house and go visit family and friends. My husband's undiagnosed OCD centered around Covid became worse. Family members and friends were becoming affected by this virus. Due to Covid-19, my anxiety increased. The month of April feels like a blur now.

The month of May approached, and I had an overwhelming of emotions. I realized I was not ok even though it took me almost the whole month to verbalize those feelings. I found myself crying in the shower and in my car when I was alone. I was sad at first. It was not a constant sadness, but I knew it could very well lead to depression. I knew at this point I had to allow my profession in the mental health field to help me, so I could help my family cope. I began using various coping skills. I would use diversions coping skills to allow myself to stop thinking about the stress induced situations. These skills consisted of taking a long hot bath, listening to music, exercising, or taking the kids on a drive. These skills worked in the beginning, but eventually I had to move towards skills to give me hope and resiliency for the future. I knew this virus was going to be a part of our lives. We had to learn to adapt to it.

After crying to myself and hiding my fears, I started using social and interpersonal coping skills by involving others. My husband started encouraging and reinsuring me that we were going to get through this "turn up" together. He began apologizing for the part he played in the stressors I was feeling daily. He started suggesting things we could do along with visiting family members. We knew we needed social support in difficult times.

Mother's Day was filled with laughter with family. Things were looking up again. Before the end of the month of May, on Memorial Day, life shifted again. Black Lives Matter was been shouted on every television and radio stations across the world. George Floyd was his name this time. The world was going mad and so was the Sewell's household. At this point, all I could think about was my two Black sons and Black daughter. I cried constantly. I prayed constantly. I was hurting for every Black mother. I feared losing my sons and daughter due to police brutality and the racial injustice in this world.

Currently, I am finding ways to think in more rational ways. I am learning ways to recognize and change irrational thoughts. I know that "all things work together for good to them that love God, to them who are the called according to his purpose." We all have a purpose just like George Floyd who is bringing the world together as one. Just like Covid-19, it made families better together. Changes are happening around us.

Never give up. Use prayer and your coping skills to deal with the "turn ups" in your life.

COVID-19
-Pamela Smith-

"I CAN'T BREATHE"
Not because the policemen has his knee on my neck
But because COVID-19 is on the prowl and it has no respect
For the young, the old, black or white, or nationality
To be in Christ and hide yourself in thee is the best place
   anyone can be

"I REALLY WANT TO BREATH"
Unfortunately there's a face mask I am forced to wear
And to go outside without, I wouldn't dare
There's a nasty virus that's called COVID-19
It's deadly, powerful; it's global and has forced us all in
quarantine
To be specific, this is the worst virus ever transpired to this
   land
Vacation, traveling, dining in restaurants, beaches, and so
   many others has been banned

"I NEED TO BREATH"
COVID-19 kills cities, destroy towns, shutdown sporting
events,
   concerts, hair salons and barber shops
This evil virus seems to be nonstop
Furthermore, Coronavirus has forced schools, Churches,
   Stores, and jobs to close and has even shut down the
   government.
Staying inside, sanitizing, and following all the rules is for the
   entire nation's betterment

"I'M TRYING SO HARD TO BREATHE"
Nevertheless, not being able to hug my family and friends and
   greet them with a kiss
This is so heartbreaking and I truly and definitely miss
Staying six feet apart and practicing social distancing, it's a
   must

This could be the new normal and we have to learn to adjust

"I STILL CAN'T BREATHE"
According, this pestilence virus is overwhelming and has killed
   a multitude
This virus comes from the pits of hell and it's extremely rude
Corono has sparked a health crisis prompting many to seek
God for comfort, strength, understanding, and peace
Praying and hoping that this pandemic will soon cease.
The price of gas went down but the price of food skyrocketed
People in a frantic buying Lysol, hand sanitizer, alcohol,
   Clorox, and there are many issues
Lord I pray that I can just find a single roll of toilet tissue
Corono has got everyone filled with so much greed
Please remember God already told us He would supply all our
   needs

"I CAN BREATHE"
COVID-19 shouldn't be a big surprise if you read God's Holy
   Word
Seek God, repent, turn from your wicked ways He will save
   you, haven't you heard?
This virus we cannot see has shut the entire world down
But there is a God that can turn this whole situation around
Although this virus is powerful and spreading over the world
God is omnipresent, omnipotent; there is nothing He can't do
Trust and believe He can see you through
There will be many plagues, tornadoes, earthquakes, fires,
   floods, volcanos, and viruses that will come to this land.
But pray without ceasing, life right, trust in God, repent daily,
   and please keep your hand in God's hand
No doubt, if we wash hands often, wear masks, stay six-feet
   apart, and stay inside as much as possible, and break these
   rules; NEVER!!!
Call out to God; take care of ourselves and each other and we
   can get through this TOGETHER!!!

-Stevetta Temple-

During 2020, so many lies were taken away due to gun violence and black on black crime, at a high rate, officers are killing young men at a heavy rate. I don't look at what's happening as strange. The Book of Revelation talked about this was going to happen. Now we are dealing with Covid-19, which I call a deadly weapon.

Working in a hospital, I have seen it all. Patients are scared, patients are dying, patients can't breathe, patients on a ventilator, not to mention their loved ones can't visit. I just believe that where there is negativity, there is always positivity.

During Covid-19, people that weren't close to their loved ones are getting closer. Their loved ones that stepped away from the relationship, with God, have gotten right back in good standings with GOD. There's a saying, "when the devil is messing, God is blessing."

Many jobs were also lost, and many got hired. The awesome thing I also see is many people became business owners. I became a business owner of two businesses; Star's Sexy Shades and Star's balloon creations. That let me know that GOD is still in control.

During these times, we got to stay focused, and most of all prayed up. The family members that had COVID-19, in my family, the Lord has seen fit to let them see another day. I'm so grateful for that.

What is important is to remember that we are all in this fight together. Let's stay true and faithful to each other. Lastly, always encourage someone else along the way. Give a hand and a hug and even a smile when need be. Thank you.

Reclaiming My Time
Finding A New Normal in the Midst of a Global Pandemic
-Tanya Thompson-

It was late January 2020 and I had just completed teaching my first series of ESL classes that particular night. I was new to the online teaching world and loved every minute of it. After all, I could travel to China daily without ever leaving the comfort of my home. I loved seeing the joy on the children's tiny faces when my computer camera opened at the beginning of each class. It seemed quite fitting to be able to use my love for the English language as a way to pour into young minds. My heart was full as I realized these young learners were gaining crucial knowledge that will one day allow them to be more comfortable speaking the English language and subsequently building friendships and relationships. How wonderful it felt to be an integral part of someone else's success.

I desperately missed the smile and laughter of young children, as my own daughter was a senior in college, so this left me as an empty nester since the ripe old age of 43. When my daughter was younger, I found great joy in watching her learn and grow. This new teaching venture was a perfect fit for my new stage in life. Though I must admit that there was a sense of fear attached to the prospects of meeting dozens of new students and families each day. I was fascinated with the idea of trying something new.

One of my older students and I had become quite comfortable speaking with one another about the differences in our two worlds. I was fascinated to learn about the Chinese New Year and the different customs. When we teach English as a second language, the pupils are free to select an English name to use during our classes together. This beloved student chose the English name Eva. Her parents chose this English name for their daughter because the Hebrew derivation means "life."

This name really fits Eva because she is truly full of hope and lives life to the fullest. She has the unique ability to find the good in almost every situation. However, this night I could sense the fear and uncertainty is my beloved student's voice.

"Teacher, many people around me are becoming sick and I am very scared." Eva was referring to the of the Corona Virus crisis in her hometown of Wuhan, China. I watched daily as her world was turned upside down, not knowing that the very same conditions would touch down in the United States and other parts of the globe very soon after.

By late February, the city of Nashville, TN had been affected by COVID-19. Schools were closed indefinitely and droves of employers ordered their employees to begin working remotely. Life as we knew it was no more. A trip to the grocery store felt more like a scavenger hunt for grocery staples and household supplies. As a diabetic, I found myself waiting in extremely long lines to have my insulin filled, only to find out that the delivery truck was late due to shipping delays. I remembered what my student's mother told me about how they prepared for remaining at home during the pandemic.

She advised that we obtain at least two months of non-perishable goods, frozen foods and household staples. She also advised that we might need to begin purchasing hand sanitizer and disinfectant spray. These items were in high demand and many did not have the necessary funds to purchase what they actually needed in order to survive. It was hard watching as the world changed daily. I remember my grandmother telling me stories of rationing measures that were taken during the Great Depression as I stood face to face with a sign that read "Limit 1 of each household cleaning item per household." As I made my way to the meat and dairy section, there was not one carton of eggs, gallons of milk or sugar to be found. I was merely a spectator because I had listened to my Chinese student's mother and purchased a two-month supply of items for our home. Yet, I was amazed at the rapid turn of events.

Then, the first week of March brought another devastating blow. The city of Nashville was hammered with an EF-4 tornado that literally wiped out many areas of the city – including our neighborhood. Our entire street was covered with trees and large debris. Many buildings were completely demolished by the unexpected force of the winds and rain. We were without internet and power for almost two weeks. Many homes were also victims of looting and violence during the darkness. God kept us covered and I am forever grateful that He saw fit to spare our lives.

Even in the midst of this extremely difficult season, God continued to show Himself mighty in our lives. Assistance with clean up and rebuilding was coming from every direction. By the time our power and internet were restored, we had received a $5,000.00 monetary blessing and we were given endless amounts of household supplies to help us get back on our feet. We were able to repair and replace items within our home and it turned out better than what we started with. I found out that God will make good on His promises to take care of His children.

God has given me so much creativity, resilience and business opportunity during this season. The year 2020 has made me realize that I can truly do all things through Christ. I now understand that He is my strength when I am weak and worn. In the past, I felt helpless when trouble arose. But I declare that I am reclaiming my time. I will take authority over every situation. I will win.

It was my turn to stand under an open heaven and it didn't matter what the obvious condition of the world around may have been, I was able to hold fast to God's promises for my life. I quickly learned that His promises are not contingent upon a news report or environmental condition. He was able to show His majesty in every situation. God blessed me in the midst of worldwide chaos and confusion. Nevertheless. I am reclaiming my time.

May we be cured, restored & totally healed from the
DISEASE OF ADDICTION TO THIS TEMPORARY LIFE

-Cece Washington-

God's Nature is Healing
"God's Nature is not sickness & disease"
Jehovah Rapha Our Healer!

GOD IS LOVE

Pandemic/Current Times, offers the grandest opportunity for total surrender to our Mighty God, our hope. Hope thou in me, says the Lord. We don't talk about Heaven enough, but that's where our Saviour Jesus sits at the right hand of the Father. Heaven is His throne, and Earth is His footstool.

I do not speak of dying. I speak of living forever, where there is no death, no sickness, no pandemic, no racial issues, no political parties, no denominations, no clicks, no evil. I speak of a place worth longing for. That does not make me ungrateful for the air I'm breathing right now, just a new perspective.

Just imagine if we were to think on those things that are lovely, that are pure, the home Jesus spoke of before ascending, after His death and resurrection. Jesus said, "I go to prepare a place for you, where I go, there you may be also."

We must believe these words and live a life unto the Lord here on earth. We must be purpose-driven, keep God's commandments, and be Holy for He is Holy. You can find the rest of the instructions as you study to show yourself approved by God. You, the workman that need not be ashamed as you rightly divide, apply, and live out the word of God that you have hidden in your heart that you may not sin against Him.

We receive the instructions, and we are walking out the instructions for the most part, but we slowly lose sight of the HOPE Jesus left for us, which is " I go to prepare a place for you, where I go there ye may be also, I will return for you. "

Imagine for a second if we were to zone in on those words. Are we longing just to live here longer? But what about an everlasting life in Heaven with God, our creator. While seeing the goodness of God in the land of the living?

I suffered an empty nest so bad for a few years, and then the "Nana Babies" started coming, which brought some relief. But now that the kids are grown, and the grandkids are gone, I face a second round of empty nest (currently happening. God is currently longing for His children. We are His children). I can't truly put it into words what I feel. I just know it does not feel good. In spite of how much my heartaches and the pain I've experienced with kids and grands, it hurt so good. I still long for them.

We are the children of God. He longs for us to be with Him, in spite of our mess. This life was designed by God but as a temporary setting. I know it hurt me so bad to see my kids fighting when they were growing up. The jealousy the envy, the bitterness, the hatred was not from me. I was not raising kids to hate each other. I wanted them to value each other, respect their differences, and simply love each other through patience for one another.

I believe God is about to do something about this temporary home. He is about to "fix all the broken things" as my nana baby, T'Lanee, would say.
I believe He is ready for us to come to our eternal home. We can put on the whole Armor of God and His Fruit of the Spirit. I mean, as I stated earlier, sickness and disease are not the nature of God. He wants us healed, set free, delivered. We have made wrongs seem right, and right seem wrong.

We have compromised His character in our lives. We say we are following hard after God-but the minute the world presents something attractive we run hard after it. So the things we ought to do we do not and the things we ought not to do we do. We are double-minded men and women, making us unstable in all of our ways. There is a way of a man that seems right, but the end thereof is death.

It's like telling my kids to clean up their mess in the living room; everybody wants to say, "I didn't do it." God sees all, and He knows all. He knows who did what, and He knows those that did not follow His instructions. Blame shifting didn't work in our house; it definitely won't work with God.

Work out your own salvation with fear and trembling, cause ain't none of His kids doing what we are supposed to be doing, like going ye therefore and teach all nations, baptizing them. What church is reaching the lost now? Instead, we're building large, colorful church boxes. To be relevant to the world rather than reverent towards God.

What I'm trying to say is, get right church and let's go home! Forgive your fellow man and "momma-nem." Your Pastor was growing with you; he/she needs Jesus too. Hey church mother, that Single mom needs your love, not your judgment. Young man, find wisdom and cling to her. Children obey your parents. Go back to your first love ministry leader. Dad, don't keep provoking your children to anger. Mom, be her friend, never her buddy. Business owners, pay your tithe, and value integrity. You'll get more bees with honey. Police officer, protect and serve as you said in your oath on that day in humility when you raised your right hand. Preachers stop using the pulpit to vent. See a therapist, seek the counsel of God. Be determined not to abuse your authority over your sheep.

Saints of God, above all things, LOVE. Pray always. Forgive 70x7. Die daily. Be not conformed to this world but be ye transformed by the renewing of your mind through daily bible reading.

Jesus will return, and every knee will bow, and every tongue will confess that He is Lord!

FROM A NURSING HOME NURSE PERSPECTIVE
-Myrtina Wimbley-Akese-

I have always promised myself that I would care for my patients to the best of my abilities. Now I am questioning what that means. As a nurse, we are already working at full capacity and working with limited help before the pandemic. Now we have been faced with making a choice between going to work or staying home to keep ourselves, as well as our family, safe from the Coronavirus.

We are getting frustrated when our job lacks coordination with the CDC on proper protocol to keep us safe and decrease the spread of the virus. We have always thought that if anyone would be prepared for this pandemic, we would. As healthcare workers, we face all kinds of adversities, so we thought this would be just like the others. But when your employers that are supposed to have your best interest at heart seem as if they don't care, it's hard for you to care. We have been working the frontlines with improper supplies and sometimes lack of supplies. My job tells us that we can just wear a surgical mask and sometimes even a mask thinner than a piece of paper. This has angered us so much. We never got an N95 mask for our employees.

We also are getting frustrated when your job is not caring about how we feel. We have asked, on several occasions, why are we keep getting admissions of potentially infected patients. They tell us that they still have to make money. We would even admit patients that were coming straight from home with unknown statuses. Our current residents would be very scared for their lives because this is their permanent home. So, we are having to reassure them with lies.

We are frustrated because, due to these circumstances, we have lost valuable employees. Now at my job, we have one who CAN take care of 20-30 patients on an 8-hour shift. This means that the patients are not getting proper care; they are being neglected. Staff is having to work 16 hours shifts multiple times a week, and the administration will still not get us any help. We are not even receiving any hazardous pay or any compensation for working like this.

This week we had ten residents to die. The EMT says that one of the patients had been dead for at least 6 hours, which was full code. So, the nurses had to do an ice–code. This pandemic has really made me want to reevaluate my career choice and my employer.

Stand Up and Be Heard!
- Keywana Wright-

Stand up and be heard with your words and your peaceful
actions.
Demand the people respect how you walk with pride and be
proud of who you are.
God created us all equal in His sight. You are beautifully made
in the image of God.
You are a royal priesthood, peculiar people who has been
called out of darkness into His light.
Your voice can ring freedom from miles away. We have power
when we can stand as one, blacks
and whites joined hand in hand, Dr. Martin Luther King Jr.
said Let Freedom Ring.
Do not act like untamed animals but let them see that we do
have home training.
Stand up and be heard, like Mr. James Brown sang, I am
Black, and I am Proud.
Our ancestors were slaves, beaten and cast down but were not
forgotten.
They picked cotton and cleaned houses just to survive on the
plantations.
Some were beaten, hanged, and eaten alive by mean dogs of
the slave owners.
Their voices rang throughout the cotton fields; Lord, I Need
You to Help Me.
Our faith always carries us on even in difficult times, we
always looked up towards God.
Just know you are somebody smart, creative, and strong, your
life matters.
Continue to climb those mountains that are before you.
Education is powerful and no one can take it from you.
Learn how to read and write, for it is important.
Dream big dreams and know it is possible for them to come
true.
Always love hard and love even when it is not reciprocated
back to you.
Love along covers a multitude of sins.

68

Continue to trust in God. Do not lose the faith. God always has
a plan. Trust His plan even
when it does not make any sense.
Stand up and be heard.
The generations after you are counting on you to pave the way.
You may be wounded or even face death along the way but
know that someone behind you is counting on you to say, I am
somebody too, my life does matter.

So today, I am standing up with my head up high towards the
sky. I am an African American
female who is proud to be who I am; strong, smart, resilient,
and I have faith like the man named
Job in the bible, who said in Job 13:15, Though he slay me, yet
will I trust in Him.

-Erica Yates-Eatmon-

I don't know where to start. As I talk to God, all I can say is, "Papa, I'm hurt!" I'm hurt to the point of anger, but Papa, I don't want the emotions from my soul to kill your Spirit. I'm drowning in a sea of cloudy thoughts that seem unforgiving. My heart needs mending right now, Papa! I can't see through the tears that I might have rest. I want to be free! Free from this pain, fear, and anxieties of this world. How can I continue to love an unlovable world that seems like it has no love for me? Am I foolish for loving when others' actions reflect the opposite towards me?

We are living in a time where if love is not being extended to us, we reciprocate those same actions in return. I'm not going to lie, family. When someone gives me anger, I definitely want to clap back. "Who do they think they are? Oh, you definitely don't know me! Don't let the look fool you." Ha, ha! My thoughts...lol. I have let my raging emotions consume me on so many occasions that sometimes all I could see was fire in my eyes. To hell with it, burn it all down! If I'm hurting, everyone around me was going to feel it too.

One day I read, in the Bible, about a man named David that had raging emotions, too. One thing I learned from David, was that though he had raging emotions, he commanded his soul to praise God through it all. "Let all that I am praise the Lord." (Psalms 103) It made me realize that though my emotions raged within me, I didn't have to let my emotions dictate my actions, and my actions should be that of what I believe.

These days it is easy to become enraged by what is happening. The question that bothers me is, does the hate we receive justify the hate we put back out? There needs to be a war cry; however, how do we cry out to be heard?

In the 2017 movie Wonder Woman, Wonder Woman herself said it best, "It's not about deserving, it's what you believe, and

---

70

I believe love." I'm so glad that I'm not judged by what I deserve but given life through love.

Jesus, who is all-powerful, came into the flesh so that we could be given life through love. Often we view love in action as a weakness. Love in action, whether you want to believe it or not, requires sacrifice and submission. Now I'm not just talking about sacrifice and submission to another human. I'm talking about these are things God has commanded us to do to come unto Him. Sacrifice that's what Jesus was. He was a sacrifice so that we might have life. This is a man that we read about that did miraculous things. He healed the unhealable, He cast out demons, and He raised the dead because He had all power in His hands. Yet, He was not objected to the oppressions of this world. As I think back, even when Jesus was born, He was being hunted to be killed because of who He was born to be, and the fear of man kicked in. (Matthew 2) Does this sound familiar? So the behavior of man we receive out of fear and hate dates back to B.C. on the timeline.

Now Jesus eventually did die on the cross, but only through His submission and only to save our lives. Jesus had the power not to have to endure the brutalities He went through, but His Father had already told Him what needed to be done. Not many of us, if any of us, would come here knowing we would die by the very hands we were sent to save. Through all of His good works, the people still saw fit to kill what they didn't understand.

Yet much like the world today. We are being killed because of fear and misunderstanding. What I admire the most about Jesus is that He did not become what feared Him. Read that again. Jesus could have done to them what they did to Him, probably even worse. Jesus chose love and asked the Father to forgive them. Hanging on the cross, Jesus prayed for the ones who crucified Him.

Now, did I say all that to say we should lay down and take what this world gives us? Not by any means. I stated all that to say we are not exempt from the injustices/crucifixions of this world, but we should not turn into the hate and fear that is given to us.

Listen, yes, we need to fight for what's right. However, we have to factor in the who, what, when, where, and how into this thing. We want them to change their mindset, and Lord knows I pray there will be a generation of harmony among us one day. Through what I have seen demonstrated through social media, the news, and even from our current president, I can't say this will be the last fight we will ever have to fight over who we were born to be.

This has been very discouraging because I am raising a little black boy and two little black girls, and I pray my heart will never have to go through the pain of them losing their lives just because of how they look. One thing I wish we would change, as a race, is to not to give someone the reality of the perception they already have of us. I refuse to demonize myself because of the actions of other people. "When hate is loud, love cannot be silent," and that love has to be demonstrated from both sides. Though there have still been acts of hate and not understanding through this all, I am grateful for the acts of love that have been shown. From some policemen marching with protestors to protestors protecting a policeman by being human shields, so that others would not harm him. These are the actions that we need to continue to build on. These are the actions that will be heard.

To the people who do not understand us, do not get us, and get our culture confused with the definitions of black in the Webster dictionary (dirty, soiled; sinister or evil; indicative of condemnation or discredit; connected with the devil; hostility or angry discontent; marked by the occurrence of disaster, etc.), know that we are more than enough. We are beautiful, smart, caring, kind, successful, leaders, and givers to our community. We are more than the color used to describe us.

CO-AUTHORS
-Contributors-

Pen It
The People's Accounts, Emotions, and Thoughts of 2020

Volume I

Rodney Beaty, Jr.

Rodney Beaty, Jr.
Spartanburg, SC

Leon Bradshaw

Leon Bradshaw is a native of Florida. Leon released his first book, Evil Expiation, in 2016. It is a page-turner that has readers sitting on the edge of every page to see what happens next. Leon released Evil Expiation in a four-part e-book series:
-Life After Sorrow
-Warning Before Destruction
-Welcome to Chaos
-Order Out of Chaos
The compilation, Evil Expiation, lead him to become a best-selling author. Most recently, Leon penned a passionate rhythmic love by releasing Passions for Tiki.

Contact authorleonbradshaw@gmail.com for booking.

Tony Harris Brooks

Tony Orlanda Harris Brooks, is a newly published author of "STILL." Her bio is listed in Marquis Who's Who in the East. She also has published poems with Iliad Press of Big Rapids Michigan and is a life-long member of The National Poetry Society. Tony Orlanda Harris Brooks, formerly known as Tony Harris, recently married Terry Edward Brooks and resides in Cottondale, AL.

She is currently employed by Waffle House as a server. She studied nursing at Iona College and business at Shelton State Community College.

Arkeshia Brown

Arkeshia Rena Brown is an inspirational/motivational writer and speaker, founder of Whispers of God on Facebook, owner of Chasing Dreams Travel Agency, and an Amazon best-selling author. She has served 15 years in the United States Navy, is a Sexual Assault Victim Advocate, and a member of Kappa Epsilon Psi Military Sorority, Incorporated. She is also a survivor of sexual abuse. Arkeshia has her Associates and Bachelor's degree in Healthcare Administration and currently pursuing a Master's degree in Journalism at Regent University.

Jakeyla Ambriel Carlton
Jakeyla Ambriel Carlton 25-year old native of Opelika, AL, currently residing in Birmingham, AL. She the founder of The Key Marketing Management Co. (The Key)

Through her business, The Key, she hopes to live out her purpose which is helping others. Her favorite bible verse is Proverbs 11:25; a generous person will prosper, those who refreshes others will be refreshed."

Jakeyla's founding quote is "it takes one second to walk away and one second to stop and help, that one second could be the difference between life and death, that could be the mirror and you could be seeing yourself GOD is not selfish so why should I only think of myself."

Shawn T. Crawford
Shawn T. Crawford, the Poetic Father, was born in Ohio and raised in the small southern town of York, Alabama. He is the author of the newly released "Medicine for Your Soul." He is chef by trade and a poet by passion. His cooking feeds the body and his passion feeds the soul. He is a hard-working father of four. The love of his children gets him through each day.

Dionne Edison
Dr. Dionne Edison is a retired educator with over 45 years of formal service. She has worked with students of all ages from

toddlers in family day care homes through higher education. She has published two books: March of the C.O.W.S: Creatures of Wonderful Simplicity a short !whimsical book of poetry and prose; and Success Beyond Academics: How to Set Expectations for Life co-authored with her daughter, Mrs. Asenath Edison-Gay, to help individuals gain the knowledge and the resources needed to assess their skills, maximize their potential, and live a life of purpose.

Brie Fash

Brie Fash (Bridget Jackson-Fasheru) 38 years of age, lives in Shreveport, LA; where she is the owner of Brie Fash, LLC. A Graphic Designer, Brand Strategist, and Apparel Designer. She is also a Member of the Sophisticated women of Sigma Tau Sigma Sorority, INC. founded in 2017 in Atlanta, GA where is she the Director of Graphic Design. Brie Fash has set out to reach young women and tell her story in hopes that it makes an impact in someone's life; as well as make her mark on the world.

Tre' Finklea

Tre' Finklea is a native of Monroeville, AL and currently resides in Tuscaloosa, AL. Tre' is married to his college sweetheart, Jessica and together they have a son, Houston and a fur baby Fancy Monroe.

Tre' attended Stillman College earning his B.S. in Biology. He then attended the University of West Alabama and received his M.Ed. in Higher Education Administration-Student affairs. He is currently attending Liberty University to obtain his Ph.D. in Higher Education Administration.

Sheila D. Green

Sheila D. Green is a certified Life Coach trained in psychology, counseling and social work. Sheila is a motivational speaker addressing marriage, family relationships and self-care awareness. She has been working in these areas for the past 20 years. She has extensive experience counseling single and married women. She is an experienced Life Coach skilled in helping to improve relationships, improve health and wellness, and helping clients to execute strategies that lead to effective outcomes and positive living. Sheila is the author of the book, "The Business of a Successful Marriage: Treating Your Marriage Like a Business." She was featured in the May issue of Onyx Magazine as a new rising author. Her second book on self-care is coming soon. Sheila is the president and CEO of SDGreen Consulting. In all of Sheila's work, she draws from her experiences of being married for over 32 years and raising two children with her husband Lee. Learn more at sdgreenconsulting.com.

Denise Hair

Denise Hair is married with two daughters. She is the Founder of D.O.T.S (Daughters of Today's Society), serves as Vice President of C.A.P.S (Child Abuse Prevention Services), and works as a Surgical Technician by day. Denise loves to encourage people and use every gift and talent God has given her all for him to receive the glory.

Laura Hurst Olave

Laura Hurst Olave grew up in a family of educators with limited financial means but boundless resourcefulness and inspiration. As the oldest of two children, she exceled academically and earned a Bachelor of Science in physics and mathematics from University of Alabama in Huntsville. Currently employed as a data analyst with a large telecommunications company, Laura loves to assist students with her work as a math tutor. In addition to being an enthusiastic and inventive home cook, she is also a passionate student of Latin dance, including salsa, bachata, and merengue.

Pamela Ray Jackson

Pamela Ray Jackson is a self-published author from Riverview, FL and a Fashion Blogger for style and empowerment. Pam strives to provide empowerment, style and personal development tips to women but laying the foundation for all to develop and grow. She is developing a professional development series to refine interview strategies to aid in job hunting success. Her biggest achievement was expanding tips and techniques for fashion and different social media platforms to encourage growth and style expression. Contact Pam at sunraisfashion@gmail.com or www.sunraisfahion.com.

Natasha Jones

Natasha Jones is the visionary and founder of Single, Saved & Satisfied, 4 Walls First, Deliverance Intercessors Rise Up, & Work the Runway Mentorship & Fashion Expo. She is the C.E.O. of Kingdom Attitude where she specializes in graphic designs, Love Ministry Life Coaching, Vocal Coaching, Mime Dance, Strategy Building Concepts, Marketing, Branding & Kingdom Apparel. She is well-known for her LIVE Facebook Ministry Sessions "Kingdom Purpose Talk" and her conference call ministry, The Love Academy. She received accreditation in 2007-2008 to effectively teach Effective Church Leadership & Effective Choral Conducting and Praise & Worship Strategies.

When she's not ministering, she can be found writing music and working in the medical field as a Physician's Assistant, X-Ray Technician & EKG Specialist Technician. She is the proud mother of three amazing daughters.

Mia Monique

Mia Monique is a published Amazon Best Selling Author, Motivational Speaker and Domestic Violence Advocate.

Mia a former victim of Domestic violence and Emotional abuse, now advocates for her community to bring awareness and healing. She works with Women, Men and Children who face the same perils she did as a child and into her adult years. Her mission is to educate victims of abuse who may suffer from traumatic childhood experiences, domestic violence, and low self-esteem. Mia Focuses on Narcissistic personality disorder and Co-DEPENDENCY.

Mia First became active in 2011 when she was the Keynote Speaker in Johnstown PA at an annual Walking in Her Shoes event. She then founded her own Organization Meaningful Impact Association (M.I.A) which helps victims of abuse. Mia's Podcast Conversation and Clarity with Mia Monique can be found on all media streaming platforms.

Cheryl D. Moore
Cheryl DuBose-Moore is a wife, mother, and sister. She has steadily progressed working in the mental health field for 16-years. She is a member of Rock City Church, Tuscaloosa, where she prides herself with serving others. Cheryl says that family ties and community growth are always focal points. Her personal motto is "just dwell."

Laqueisha Prince
Laqueisha Prince Tuscaloosa, Alabama
Email: laqueishaprince35@gmail.com
Website: https://linktr.ee/MrsAlabama1

Cynthia Sewell
Cynthia Sewell is 47 years old, a wife of 20 years to an amazing and loving husband, and mother to a beautiful, smart and intelligent Queen. She is a Medical Billing Specialist with 13 years of experience in the medical field.

Cynthia attended the Livingston University (presently University of West Alabama). She has a passion for people. Working in the medical field has allowed her to meet so many people of different ethnic backgrounds and social statuses. It has opened her eyes and heart to show compassion and love for everyone. She states, "You never know who you will come across that just needs a warm smile and to just hear, 'Everything will be okay. The world needs more love for one another, to heal and live truly as one nation under God.'"

DeAndrae R. Sewell

DeAndrae Rashad Sewell, Sr. was born in Marengo County, Alabama. He is married to Mrs. Lakisha Sewell and has three children Jeremy, Yasmine, and DeAndrae II. He has been a member of Kappa Alpha Psi Fraternity, Inc. for 17 years. He graduated from the University of West Alabama with a degree in History and Political Science. Also, he has a master's degree in Guidance and Counseling. He is employed by the State of Alabama and a Non-Profit Program where his role is a Counselor and a Marriage and Healthy Relationships Educator. Mr. Sewell is a Deacon at St. Peter Baptist Church in Linden, AL. He enjoys volunteering his time and spreading awareness with his wife as a Co-Founder of Strive Outreach.

Debbie Lynn Sewell

Debbie Lynn Sewell. I was born and raised in the town of Linden, Alabama which is in Marengo County. I am the third child in a family of eight children. I have been employed with the Marengo County Health Department for 30 years. I received my bachelor's degree in Human Services with a minor in Psychology from Alabama State University in 1984. I am a member of St. Peter Missionary Baptist Church in Linden, Alabama where I serve as Sunday School Secretary, Church Announcer, President of the Missionary Department, and member of the church choir. My goal in life has always been to look for the good in everyone spread peace and harmony.

LaKisha Sewell, M.S

Mrs. LaKisha Sewell is the mother of three and married to Deacon DeAndrae R. Sewell Sr. She is a member of St. Peter Baptist Church where she serves as a Deaconess. She has a Master of Science in Counseling and Psychology from The University of West Alabama. Her undergraduate degrees are in psychology and sociology from The University of West Alabama as well. She worked within the mental health population for over a decade. She serves as a Program Coordinator of a Rehabilitative Day Program and a CPR/EFA Instructor in Tuscaloosa, Alabama. She is Founder of STRIVE Outreach, LLC. She spends time researching and coordinating many projects that consist of women spirituality, sickle cell anemia, mental health, and breast cancer awareness. Also, Lakisha is a co-Author of "Sisters to Sisters Daily Inspirational" and "Mom, Why Do I" Children Activity Book, she wrote with her 9 year old son, De'Andrae. Most recently, Lakisha is a co-Author in "Queens Supporting Queens Anthology." She is a licensed Cosmetologist which facilitated the desire to help people in need.

Pamela Smith

Pamela Smith enjoys writing poetry. She is a wife, a mother of our and a grandmother of nine and soon to be great grandmother. Her poetry honors God's blessing in her life.

Stevetta Temple

Elder Stevetta Temple is originally from Detroit Michigan and now resides in Tuscaloosa, Alabama for over 10 years. She's a prayer warrior and has been in ministry for over 20 years. Stevetta is a health care worker at DCH Medical Center. She is also an author, actor, and business owner,

Most of all Elder Temple loves the Lord. Her favorite scripture is Psalms 122:1; I was glad when they said until me let us go into the house of the Lord. Stevetta is the loving mother of seven children.

Tanya Thompson

Evangelist Tanya Thompson is an African-American author, singer/songwriter who hails from Nashville, TN. She is the mother of one daughter, Mikayla Thompson, a senior at Tennessee State University. Evangelist Tanya is the author of ten solo books and four anthologies. She is the CEO and Founder of Glory After the Rain Publishing House, where she teaches writing courses and offers book publishing support. Glory After the Rain Ministries, where she hosts an early morning devotional show that reaches people across America and into International waters. In her daily walk, Tanya serves as a Utilization Review Nurse for a large healthcare firm in Franklin, TN. Evangelist Tanya is pursuing a dual enrollment program for her Master and PhD in Theological Studies. She enjoys reading, writing, and spending time with her family.

Cece Washington

Cece Washington is married to Alex Washington since 1990, they met in Alex's northern hometown in 1985. They went down South to start fresh with their four children just a few days after saying "I Do". She unapologetically raves about her eight "nana babies" very often in conversation. A good number of single moms that she has ministered to, still refers to her as their spiritual mom.

She is the Founder and CEO/Director at Beyond the Altar Ministries, a 22 year old ministry birthed in 1998, however, just becoming a 501©3 Non-Profit Tax Exempt Organization on July 14, 2020. She is honored to be recognized by her Pastor, Dr. Scott Schatzline since 2018, as a Para-Mission Minister/ Home Missionary. A missionary in and to her own community, a minister of reconciliation to one "homeless working single mom family" at a time. However, ministering to the needs of all people "Beyond the Altar" she continues to serve as a Pastoral Care Worker at Daystar Family Church in Northport Alabama This has been her family's home church since 1993 under the leadership of Dr. Scott Schatzline and founder/spiritual dad, Bishop Patrick Schatzline. Cece continues to serve as a chaplain at the local hospitals.

Prior leadership roles include active membership for the Tuscaloosa Salvation Army Women's Auxiliary as Fundraising Coordinator and chaplain for The Good Samaritan Clinic of Tuscaloosa, for many years Cece offered spiritual counseling by private referral to many women that visited a local health clinic.

She launched BTA Institute on May 22, 2019 where she now serves as Chancellor while simultaneously studying to receive a Doctorate of Theology. Cece is the proud author of "Tennis Wife" published in 2016 and many other unwritten books, as she often states. Cece loves to worship, pray and read the word. Hosting Bible Studies brings her much joy. In her free time Cece loves to paint, create DIY projects and repurpose common use household items. Most items are given away as she ministers "Beyond the Altar."

Much of the aforementioned events and information took place after she suffered a stroke in 2008, paralyzing her left side. However, Cece continues to "go on to live victoriously" serving God and spreading JOY wherever she goes. She always looks for the light in every dark situation bringing hope to each one she meets, all to the glory of God. Praise ye the Lord! Hallelujah!

Mry'Tina Wimbley-Akese
Mry'Tina Wimbley-Akese is a mother of three college students from Madison, AL. She has been a home health and geriatric nurse for 17 years. She is proud to be a professional and dedicated Black woman in the field of nursing. She's very compassionate about the needs and welfare of her patients. Also, she serves as the Community Director of Strive Care which focus on the care of teen moms during their pregnancy.

Keywana Wright

Keywana Wright is a native of Flint, Michigan. She is a devoted mother of one daughter, Miss Tayler Williams. Ms. Wright is a self-publisher and author of the three short devotional books, "Walking in God's Destiny", "Keywana's Collection of Prayers and Poems", and "31 daily prayers for the Virtuous woman". She is a Motivational speaker, Writer, Certified Life Coach and Prayer Warriors. She hosts a podcast program "Good Night Prayers with Keywana Wright" on Tuesday's at 9pm.

Keywana is a Jr. Missionary and serves in various capacities at her local church as well as the community. Keywana's dream is to work and serve in full-time women's outreach ministry. She has a God-giving love for women and to help them reach their purpose in the Kingdom of God. She believes in the power of prayer. She is a witness that there is nothing impossible to him that believe.

Over the past 14 years she has continued to work in the Human Service Field. She also has worked with domestic Violence and sexual assault victims. She is a volunteer at Carriage Town Ministries and Building Strong Women transitional housing. She encourages and uplifts the women to become their best.

Keywana holds a Bachelor of Arts degree in Family Life Education from Spring Arbor University. She recently received a certificate in Leadership in Ministry. Certified Life Coach Keywana's favorite bible verse, "In all thy ways acknowledge him and he shall direct thy path. Proverbs 3:6

Erica Yates-Eatmon

I am 36 years old from Butler, AL in Choctaw County. I currently reside in Tuscaloosa, AL with my wonderful husband and three wonderful children. I am a mental health professional with 13 years of experience in intellectual/developmental disabilities and mental illness. I received my bachelors degree in Psychology and my masters degree in Counseling/Psychology from the University of West Alabama. My passion is to advocate and support for the world to see the value and great abilities in all not just a few.

About the Visionary
-Pam Ryans-

Ms. Pamela (Pam) Ryans is a native of York, Alabama; a resident of Lyman, South Carolina; and is an avid author and empowerment speaker who provide her audiences with captivating and powerful life messages. Her illustrious career began at a reflecting point as she struggled to find her identity in the midst of silence.

Ms. Ryans formalized her education through attendance at Stillman College, a Historically Black College. In pursuit of her purpose, she chose to drop her studies during her senior year. Returning to Stillman ten years later, she completed her Bachelor's Degree in Business Administration with a concentration in Marketing. Pam continued her studies and obtained a Master's Degree in Counseling and Psychology from the University of West Alabama.

In the midst of a diverse and vast life, Pam Ryans is the Founder of "1 Vision Empowerment," where she a life coach and publisher. Through "1 Vision Empowerment," she is the Founder of the Stillman College Alumni Authors Book Dedication and founder of the Books and Brews Author's Showcase. She also provides academic and career workshops for students of all ages. Pam provides inspirational ministry encouragement via "Transform Your Mind with Pam Ryans," (text, email, YouTube videos, and on Facebook). Pam dedicated her personal time, as a caregiver to her mother, who battled Stage IV breast cancer until her recent passing. Through her dedication and an intense desire to support other caregivers, Pam began a organization entitled "The Daughter of Sarah". Pam hosts an annual event for the organization and provides gifts to caregivers. Additionally, the program advocates the importance of early detection of all illnesses and an awareness of the family history.

Pam pens her life's journey and is a bestselling author. Unselfishly, Pam is also publisher of other #1 bestselling authors.

Most proudly, Pam mothers four amazing young ladies and is the grandmother of four joys of her life. Her interest is expressing love through knowledge, correction, and expression. She enjoys cooking, music, reading, and just laughing at and with herself and friends.

Her books and services are available at **www.pamryans.com**.